POCKET IMAGES

Herefordshire

Racking a barrel of cider outside the New Inn, Pembridge, c. 1880. Produced at a local farm the barrel is receiving every care and attention.

POCKET IMAGES

Herefordshire

Anne Sandford

NONSUCH

For William

First published 1992
This new pocket edition 2007
Images unchanged from first edition

Nonsuch Publishing
Cirencester Road, Chalford
Stroud, Gloucestershire, GL6 8PE
www.nonsuch-publishing.com

Nonsuch Publishing is an imprint of NPI Media Group

British Library Cataloguing in Publication Data.
A catalogue record for this book is available from the British Library.

ISBN 978-1-84588-419-2

Typesetting and origination by NPI Media Group
Printed in Great Britain

Contents

An old lady at her doorway in the Back Lane, Ledbury. Originally called de Halle-ende, these seventeenth-century cottages were demolished in the late 1960s and the road was straightened. This fine group of houses is depicted here in around 1900.

The Trumpet Inn, c. 1905. A popular stopping point for refreshment for both cyclists and wagons, it was for many years an old coaching inn known as the Original Trumpet Inn. The landlord was James Townsend, beer retailer and shopkeeper.

Introduction

This collection of photographs dates from around 1860 to the 1940s and reflects the subjects considered to be of greatest interest to both the amateur and professional photographers of the time. One of the smallest counties of the West Midlands, Herefordshire is compact, with the City of Hereford at its centre. Many photographs of the city survive, but life in the towns and villages was fully captured, and it is these records which give the observer a glimpse of the various facets and intensity of life in earlier times. People disport themselves in leisure activities or pose proudly with the tools of their trade or with their prize livestock. Fine country houses, some now rubble or grassy mounds, take their place with theatrical and political events in the rich panoply of local life. The changes in the landscape, both town and country, over the last eighty to a hundred years are many, and photography is perhaps the most telling record of them that we have.

As an area of great natural beauty, then as now, Herefordshire has always inspired photographic endeavour. We are fortunate that many negatives and prints produced by the antiquarian and pioneer photographer, Alfred Watkins (of *The Old Straight Track* fame), remain in the City Library, as well as the painstaking records of F.C. Morgan made in the 1920s and '30s. The work of professional photographers such as W.H. Bustin of Palace Yard, Preece, Wilson, Ladmore and Unwin, with many others, is available at the County Record Office and in the city museums' collections. Pioneer photographers also produced photographic postcards and Tilley of Ledbury is perhaps the prime exponent. However, although much work by photographers of the period has disappeared, there always remains the possibility and hope that it will, at some time, be discovered; and probably in the most unexpected and unlikely places! In producing this book, many treasures have been unearthed in attics, barns and long forgotten family albums.

I trust that this compilation of photographs of our county and its activities of former years will produce as much pleasure for you as its research and assembly has for me.

Westfield House, Holly Bush, near Ledbury.

Teatime at Westfield House, Hollybush, near Ledbury in 1905.

One

Hidden Herefordshire

An early view towards Garway church and farm, showing the dome-roofed dovecot dating from c. 1326 and built by the Knights Hospitallers.

Above: The stark tower of Garway church dates from the thirteenth century, and is linked by a seventeenth-century corridor to the late thirteenth-century nave on a different axis. A community of the Knights Templars was founded here around 1180; the tower had originally been isolated and the church was formed with a round nave and chancel.

Left: An early photograph of the piscina in the south chapel in Garway church. These curious carvings, including the fish and the snake, and winged chalice and wafer, have always excited much speculation and may have a Knights Templar connection. Some people think, though, that the carvings are later than the fourteenth century.

The south doorway at Kilpeck, a favourite subject of many Victorian photographers. The late Georgian gravestones are somewhat more weathered today, but the doorway is still a remarkable sight in superb condition. The tree of life tympanum, the birds, dragons and beak heads are still crisp and sumptuously carved. The two splendid soldiers with ribbed clothing and the hideous dragons writhe on the jambs. The church was probably built in the second quarter of the twelfth century and there are many similarities with Shobdon, thought to be of similar date. The centrepiece of the Herefordshire School of Sculpture, all facets of carving at Kilpeck have been analysed. The native craftsmanship in the country must have helped in the creation of such vital and exuberant work.

Alfred Watkins's splendid photograph of the corbel table at Kilpeck church. One of the most perfect Norman churches in England, it has been called the jewel of the county. A few gaps indicate the removal of corbels by the Victorians, whose sensibilities were offended by the erotic nature of some of the subjects. One did escape their ministrations, however, a 'sheila-na-gig', a female fertility symbol.

This view of Kilpeck has not changed for at least 800 years. The dragon heads at the corners project at corbel level like the ships' figureheads of the Vikings.

Above: This fine arch at Brinsop church, photographed in 1904, is another example of the superb Norman carvings (c. 1150–60) to be found in Herefordshire churches. Similar to Rowlstone church, these arches depict human figures, animals and a fine Sagittarius. The tympanum of St George in this church was also much photographed by the Edwardians.

Right: Alfred Watkins's splendid detailed photograph of Eardisley font taken in 1930 shows another example of the Hereford school of Norman carving. The figures of the two fighting knights are brilliantly captured together with the Harrowing of Hell. The figures are very like those at Kilpeck, and the carving of Christ is similar to the figures on the chancel arch there.

The Norman arch at Rowlstone church, a fine example of the Herefordshire School of Sculpture, perhaps second only to Kilpeck and a favourite subject for early photographers. The sculptor has used the cockerel symbol over and over again.

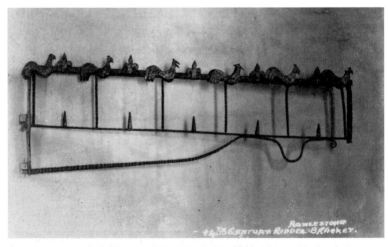

An early postcard of one of the two fifteenth-century riddel brackets in the chapel of Rowlstone church. Made of wrought iron, the birds and fleur-de-lys are a very rare survival. Each has five prickets for candles. The birds are either cockerels or swans, but cockerels seem more appropriate, as the church is dedicated to St Peter.

The east end of Craswell Priory after excavations in 1904 by C.J. Lilwall. Craswell Priory is one of only three houses of the Grandmontine order in England. Watkins's pictures of the excavations in 1904 and his further photographs in 1908 are a wonderful record of the site which has suffered considerably since the excavation. It is hoped that the site will be consolidated in the near future as much of it has not been disturbed, due to its remoteness.

The memorials appear amongst the vegetation at Bullingham old church in 1928. Today the modern church nearby contains a thirteenth-century coffin lid originally from this building, now a romantic ruin.

Above: The seventeenth-century box pews at Cloddock church recorded by Alfred Watkins in 1917, before restoration. Some of the pews date from 1660 and 1668. The church also retains a fine triple pulpit and a rare three-sided communion rail, also of the seventeenth century. The important ninth-century funerary slab, which is dedicated to the beloved wife of Guinndas, can still be seen behind the pulpit.

Below: A splendid early photograph of a medieval misericord in Canon Pyon church. The fox – one of a group of splendid animals in the church – has a goose firmly between his teeth. Even in the stalls one can find a carving of two bishops back to back between two monkeys!

This is one of the most interesting tombs in Herefordshire, dedicated to Blanche Parry, Maid of Honour to Queen Elizabeth I, who kneels here next to her Queen. Possibly carved by a follower of John Gilden of Hereford, the tomb contains Blanche's heart, brought back to her home village while her body was buried in Westminster in 1589. She was born at Newcourt, Bacton, in 1508 and entered the young Princess Elizabeth's service, becoming eventually the Keeper of Her Majesty's Jewels, and later Chief Gentlewoman of the Privy Chamber. Present at the Queen's Coronation, in scarlet and crimson velvet and cloth of gold, she was a much regarded confidante and friend of the Queen.

The Leominster ducking stool, placed in the priory church. It was last used in 1813 by Sarah Leek, who was wheeled around the town but not ducked, as the water was too shallow! This punishment was for 'scolds, nagging women and sellers of short measure or adulterated foodstuffs'. Leominster also had a whipping post and stocks, kept in the Corn Market, and a pillory in Church Street, east of the old prison. The stocks were last used in 1849 by James Morgan, a drunk who had not paid his fine.

Above: The discovery of the Roman road at Abbeydore in 1908. The road was approximately 13 ft wide with tracks approximately 4 ft 6 in wide. G.H. Jack, the County Surveyor for Hereford and a keen archaeologist, found nails and a fragment of horseshoe, and also a piece of iron which was thought to have been a heavy linchpin.

Left: The Roman tessellated pavement at Kenchester, the Roman town of *Magna*, or *Magnis*, in 1912. Part of this fine pavement is mounted on the stairs of the City Museum and Art Gallery at Broad Street, Hereford. First excavated in the 1840s by Dean Merewether, excavations took place in 1912–13, and in 1924–5 they were directed by Mr G.H. Jack. The findings were published by the Woolhope Naturalists Field Club. The small market town, of some 22 acres, was prosperous between AD 250 and AD 350, and was the economic centre of the surrounding countryside.

The circular foundations of Garway church nave, photographed by Alfred Watkins after excavation. The Knights Templars often built round churches in memory of the Holy Sepulchre in Jerusalem. The existing chancel arch belongs to the round nave, and this displays eastern, almost oriental, influences in its carving. Traces of these foundations can still be seen by the church today. Herefordshire is lucky to have two of the known round church sites in England; the other was at St Giles's, Hereford.

The Poet's Stone at Leysters commemorates the visit of the Lakeland poet William Wordsworth and his wife to Bockleton Vicarage, to stay with the Revds J. and T.E. Miller. Lying on the road between the Church House, Leysters, and Wilden, the stone marks the spot where the two Wordsworths sat and admired the view on 22 October 1845. The Millers later had their initials cut on the stone. A frequent visitor to Herefordshire, Wordsworth spent many happy hours at Brinsop Court together with his family and friends, including Southey and Edward Quillinan. He wrote many sonnets in the county inspired by aspects of the landscape, and according to William Evans, the gardener at Brinsop Vicarage for over fifty years, he was often seen 'mooning about the lanes'.

The packhorse bridge at Risbury, Humber. It is still to be seen in a field, but is very overgrown.

Alfred Watkins's fascinating photograph of the Queen's Stone at Huntsham was taken in 1926 during the excavations arranged by him. This photograph shows the depth of the excavated stone. Ploughing has reduced the amount visible today and the vertical grooves are about 2 in wide and up to 7 in deep. All the grooves stopped abruptly at the then ground level, and about 8 ft of the stone is buried. Within the excavations fragments of burnt bone, worked flints and a large amount of charcoal were found. Watkins decided that this marker stone was also a sacrificial stone, and thought that wooden rods could have been placed in each groove to form a cage or basket, perhaps bound with withies. He then proposed that a sacrificial object would have been placed in the cage and then burnt. Seven years later, at a camp of the Woodcraft Folk who were camped by the Queen's Stone, a suitable cage was built and two 'victims' were placed inside. This event was filmed and proves fascinating today. The stone was very much part of Watkins's leyline theory, as it was a marker stone for three separate alignments of the leylines (ancient trackways).

Blackfriars preaching cross at Hereford with the ruins of the monastery in the background, c. 1900. Corporal John Vernall, a Coningsby pensioner in his red coat, completes the picture. He lived in the Coningsby almshouses nearby, and as Corporal was paid £20 per year and was allowed to marry. Corporal Vernall's son also eventually became a Corporal pensioner. Corporal Vernall is shown on Edwardian commemorative china, labelled 'The Red Coat Man'.

Hay Mill at Downton was a favourite site for painters. Built in the seventeenth century, it was extended after 1784 when it was painted by Thomas Hearne. He also painted it adorned with flower pots and birdcages. The mill was still working up to around 1918 but has been demolished since.

Above: A wagon rests outside St Dubricius's church, Hentland, at the turn of the century. These men would probably have taken part in the ancient pax cake ceremony held on Palm Sunday, when bread was passed round the congregation and the words 'peace and goodfellowship' and 'peace and good neighbourhood' were spoken. This was a time when neighbours settled their differences and prepared themselves for Easter.

Right: The fine seventeenth-century ceiling in the Old Mayors Parlour Gallery at Nos 23-4 Church Street, Hereford. It was the home of Mayor Lawrence in 1627, and it is he who is supposed to have ordered the ceiling mouldings, including the city's arms.

An ancient retainer enters the fine late fourteenth-century gatehouse at Gillow Manor, Hentland, which is approached by a causeway over the moat. The gatehouse and chapel remain today as part of the partially moated farmhouse.

This strange statue at Gillow Manor, Hentland, is carved in stone and has been dated to around 1430. The 4 ft tall figure (in civilian costume) is thought to have been one of several placed on the embattled gatehouse, which is similar to those found on castles in the north of England.

Goodrich Castle gateway almost disappearing under vegetation, like Sleeping Beauty's castle, in the late nineteenth century. Today restored, and still undergoing survey and restoration, the castle was once a port of call for eighteenth- and nineteenth-century visitors when its romantic and picturesque aspects were much admired.

Opposite above: The timber-framed rear of Fawley Court, Fawley, in the late nineteenth century. The timber framing indicates its early sixteenth-century origin, but the front is of stone, about 1630. The house was built by the Gwillim family, and was purchased in the seventeenth century by Sir John Kyrle. It eventually passed into the Money-Kyrle family.

Opposite below: The interior of Fawley Court early this century. The matching settles in front of the fire seem cosy if a little uncomfortable for lengthy conversations. The rug on the back of the settle was probably much needed to keep out draughts!

The gatehouse at Brampton Bryan Castle, c. 1903. This fourteenth-century gatehouse was built by Sir Robert Harley, who married Margaret, the last of the Bramptons, in 1309. In 1643, Lady Brilliana Harley defended the castle against Royalist forces for seven weeks but eventually in vain, for five months after she died the castle was seized and destroyed. A new house was built to the south-west of the ruins in 1663 and her descendant, the 4th Earl of Oxford, built the brick and stone Brampton Bryan Hall in 1748. Today the castle remains, still owned by the Harley family, overlook the peaceful grounds, a witness to a turbulent past.

Above: The Russian Cottage on a peaceful evening at Bridge Sollars, c. 1900. This interesting building was in the Dingle on the Garnons Estate. Built between 1830 and 1840, it appears to have been a picturesque wooden 'folly', possibly used as a shelter while one was out shooting. Demolished early this century, its companion, the Swiss Cottage, still exists on the estate.

Right: The seventeenth-century lock up or prison, which adjoins the White Lion Inn at Bridstow. The city museum has a print by T.M. Webb which shows two soldiers dragging a prisoner across Wilton Bridge, possibly from this prison, towards Ross-on-Wye.

Above: The seventeenth-century hall at Pembridge Castle, c. 1918, giving a rare glimpse of an earlier life in a border castle.

Left: An early postcard of Pembridge Castle, with its partially surviving moat. Dating from the thirteenth century, the round tower is the oldest part of the building. The hall is seventeenth century, but the outer wall is part of the thirteenth-century curtain wall. The castle was at one time owned by Sir Walter Pye, and was severely damaged in the Civil War. In the eighteenth century a member of the Scudamore family lived there, and it was bought by Sir Joseph Bailey in the nineteenth century. The castle was restored in 1914 by Doctor Hedley Bartlett, and the fine sixteenth-century chapel was furnished to accommodate the Greek Orthodox rite.

Right: The tomb of St John Kemble in Welsh Newton churchyard. The stone is marked 'JK dyed the 22 August Anno Do. 1679'. In 1678 Father John Kemble was living at Pembridge Castle as chaplain to the Scudamores. He was arrested for saying Mass, which he had done throughout the country for fifty-four years. Although over 80 years old, he was taken to London for questioning and returned with great suffering to Hereford. Later sentenced to death, he was hanged on Widemarsh Common. Father Kemble's remains were reverently buried here, apart from his hand, which was severed when his head was cut off, and was hidden away as a relic.

Below left: An early postcard of a painting showing the martyrdom in 1679 of Father John Kemble in St Francis Xavier's church, Broad Street, Hereford. He was beatified in 1926 and canonized by Pope Paul VI on 25 October 1970.

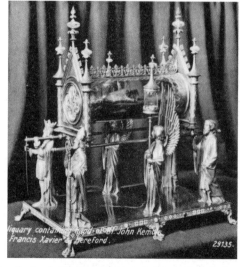

Above right: The fine reliquary containing the hand of St John Kemble in St Francis Xavier's church. His hand was cut off at his execution and concealed for many years. It had been carefully dried, and was given by a descendant of the lady who rescued it to Father Anderton SJ in 1806.

The Stoke Edith fire engine with the estate workers who formed the fire fighters: Mr R. Griffiths, with the hose, accompanied by Messrs Lewis, Baker, Webster, Cooke and Powell.

The Stoke Edith Park new steam fire engine, which replaced the old manual engine shown above.

Above: The fine mansion, Stoke Edith Park, c. 1905. It was built in the late seventeenth century by the Foley family, who employed Sir James Thornhill to paint the ceilings, staircase and the upper part of the hall with mythological figures. Isaac Bayly painted the lower panels with grotesque rocky landscapes in 1705. Sadly they were all destroyed in a disastrous fire in December 1927. The house was gutted, but the shell was rebuilt as it was intended to restore the house. The plans, however, were abandoned in the 1950s. The early eighteenth-century stables still survive. The Foley family bought and renovated the Old Rectory nearby, and some of the contents of the house which had been saved were restored and installed there.

Below: Lady Emily Foley of Stoke Edith Park strolls with her companion on Sunday 14 June 1899. They always walked to church nearby, accompanied by a footman.

The intricate parterre at Stoke Edith Park, laid out by Nesfield in 1854.

This enormous fantasy building, Goodrich Court, was designed by Edward Blore for Sir Samuel Rush Meyrick in 1828. Sir Samuel, an antiquarian and collector of armour, wished to house his collections in a suitable setting, so the house was inspired by castles on the continent that he had seen on his Grand Tour. The fantastically turreted and castellated court caused controversy, Wordsworth calling it an 'impertinent structure'. After Meyrick's death in 1848 the court was altered, partly to an Elizabethan style. Only the eastern gatehouse survives today as the court was demolished in 1950, Meyrick's fine collections long dispersed.

The Crown at Bosbury was the home of the Harford family in the sixteenth century. This postcard, dated 1921, shows the fine oak room with its large six-light transomed windows, and panelling dated 1571. The fine overmantel is one of the most ornate in the county. Some members of the Harford family are buried in the church nearby, with tombs by John Gildon of Hereford, one dated 1573 and the other 1579. Richard and Martha Harford, buried in the later sarcophagus, possessed a fine refectory table in their home, and this can be seen today in the hall of the Old House, Hereford, their initials hidden in the carving.

An interior view of Eastnor Castle, in 1902, showing the drawing room, originally the dining room, which was designed and furnished by A.W.N. Pugin around 1850. The grand chimney-piece, coved ceiling and fan vaults are spectacular, and the two-tiered Gothic chandelier is remarkable. This room featured in the BBC series The Pallisers which was filmed here. Incidentally, the writer of the card means Somers, not Somerset, in her message.

Superb carvings, thought to be by Grinling Gibbons, at Holme Lacy House, near Hereford. These carvings, including marvellous garlands, formed a vital part of the overmantels in the dining room, library and saloon. A quantity of this woodwork left the house after Sir Robert Lucas-Tooth bought the house from the 10th Earl of Chesterfield in 1910. Some carvings went to Kentchurch Court, and others may be seen in the Metropolitan Museum, New York. Today the house is for sale, and awaits the next phase in its long and varied history.

The magnificent yellow dining room at Holme Lacy House, c. 1905, before the sale of the house by Lord Chesterfield to Sir Robert Lucas-Tooth. The superb plasterwork, delicate carvings by Grinling Gibbons and rich carpets give us an idea of the glory of the house in its heyday.

TYBERTON COURT

Above: The interior of Tyberton Court at Tyberton was designed by John Wood of Bath for William Brydges in 1729, when he was only 24 years old. The Brydges family married into the Lee Warner family, which remained in the house until around 1950, but sadly the house was demolished in 1952. The last of the Lee Warner family died in 1990, and the family portraits returned to their native county in a bequest to Hereford City Museum.

Left: The wonderful Charles II state bed, which was lot 369 in the auction of the contents of Holme Lacy. Knight Frank and Rutley held the sale on 31 January 1910, by direction of the Earl of Chesterfield.

A romantic view from Clifford Castle, 150 ft above the River Wye. This was one of the fine Herefordshire castles given by the Conqueror to William FitzOsborn, and it had a long and chequered history. Owned by the Cliffords, it was the birthplace of Jane Clifford, 'Fair Rosamund', mistress of Henry II. Her tragic story is immortalized in Tennyson's *Dream of Fair Women*. Later owned by the Mortimers the castle was destroyed by Glyndwr in 1402, but the ruins today still indicate the castle's strength and dominant position.

The Jones family of White House Farm, Tupsley, outside David Cox's cottage in Baynton Wood, Tupsley, overlooking the Lugg Meadows. This cottage, originally known as George Cottage, was the home of David Cox, the artist, between 1815 and 1817. Cox came to Hereford as drawing master at Miss Croucher's Academy in Widemarsh Street, Hereford, at the end of 1814. Sadly the cottage was burned down in 1923, and many of the trees surrounding the cottage have now been felled. Mr and Mrs Morgan were living at the cottage at the time of the fire and alerted White House Farm to which the cottage belonged. The fire brigade arrived as soon as possible but the cottage was too far gone to be saved.

Above: An early twentieth-century photograph of the gatehouse at The Buttas, Kings Pyon, used here for farm storage. Dated 1632, the gatehouse has a splendid carved bressumer (a beam supporting the front of the building) and ornate barge-boards.

Left: The interior of the dovecot at Garway, in which the date 1326 is carved.

Two

People, Places and Work

This photograph of Wilton Bridge, sent in 1934, shows the eighteenth-century sundial built by Jonathan Barrow in 1718. On it was the inscription:

Esteem thy precious time
Which pass so swift away
Prepare thee for eternity
And do not make delay.

The bridge was built in 1599 and has been the main access road to Ross ever since, but during the Civil War one arch at the far end was blown up for defensive purposes, as also happened at Hereford.

A fascinating glimpse into the entrance of the Green Man Inn at Fownhope, c. 1900. The original timber-framed wall was given a brick front, possibly in the early nineteenth century when fashion dictated that brick was best. However, in the 1960s the brick was resurfaced with timber frame, giving a 'sandwich' effect. The famous prize fighter Tom Spring was once landlord here.

A late nineteenth-century view of Fownhope. The two simple thatched cottages on the left have been demolished. Note the lack of windows: presumably the cottages were cool in summer and warm in winter. One of the cottages was the communal wash-house.

Next to the churchyard wall we find the Fownhope stocks and whipping post. A reminder of savage retribution in a harsher age, although some might argue that the punishment fitted the crime! Today the stocks remain under an iron cover, placed over them in 1909 by public subscription.

Kingstone forge, in the left foreground, is still there today but the house joined on to it, called the Corner House, was pulled down in the 1950s. Part of the fine timber framing of this house was used when the forge was modernized and extended. The Bullring and the church can be seen in the distance. This photograph was probably taken by Miss Knight, daughter of the rector of Kingstone and Thruxton, who was the incumbent between 1905 and 1917.

Rose Cottage, Kingstone, photographed by Miss Knight, before the First World War. Built in the seventeenth century, Rose Cottage was also called the Tin House in later years because of its corrugated iron roof. Occupied by the Seall family from about 1840, the family were also at the Bullring and were carpenters, innkeepers, shopkeepers and tailors. The cottage was recorded by the Royal Commission and was demolished in around 1960.

A tranquil scene in the hamlet of Perton, c. 1906. This card was one of many sold at Stoke Edith post office.

Buckenhill Manor, Bromyard, home of the Tomkyns family from the early eighteenth century until 1804, when it was purchased by Robert Higginson and passed to the Barnaby Lutley family. Photographed by Bennett of Bromyard, this postcard was sent in May 1914, and reflects the tranquillity of the county just before the turmoil of the First World War.

Peaceful Ombersley village photographed c. 1906. Sent from Ledbury, this postcard was written to a favourite aunt. The correspondent hopes that the basket arrived safely, but 'no pig this year so got the spare rib on purpose for you, knowing your weakness for it.'

The Somers Arms, Eastnor, c. 1905. This delightful inn was much used by cyclists on tours in the Edwardian period. The landlord was Francis James, but although the Somers Arms was recorded as a public house in the 1860s, by 1900 it had become a temperance hotel and boarding house. Today it is a private house.

Eastnor Castle in 1905, designed by Sir Robert Smirke for the first Earl Somers. Smirke also designed the Shire Hall in Hereford and, among other buildings, the British Museum. Designed in 1812, the building contains many Victorian rooms, and even in the Edwardian period postcards of the castle were available in the village for holiday-makers to purchase. Occasionally the castle was opened to visitors as it is today.

Garnons, Mansell Gamage, in 1908, home of the Cotterell family. This photographic postcard, however, was sent by a nursemaid of the Cotterell children, signing herself Kate. On her note to her mother she says that 'the crosses mark the position of the Day Nursery', where she worked, but the Night Nursery was not in the photograph.

Above: The imitation Jacobean lodge at Brockhampton Court, Brockhampton by Ross in 1905. This card was sent by a maid called Lizzie to her mother, Mrs Hall of Lugwardine, asking for her aprons to be sent on. She also said that the lodge was the butler's house, presumably linked to the main house by a suitable bell system.

A group of pensioners at Stoke Edith hamlet in June 1915. The hamlet was the area of Stoke Edith where the pensioners on the estate lived in a group of cottages specially for their use. The splendid group here is as follows: Back row, left to right: George Lewis (80), William Webster (86), Edward Cook (69), Preb. W.H. Lambert (81). Front row: Sarah Anne Lewis (76), Mrs Lambert (73), Mary Anne Cooke (76), Ann Mellin (79), Elizabeth M'Carthy (89).

Opposite below: The outdoor staff at Stoke Edith Park c. 1900 comprised fourteen men and two women. The women did weeding and looked after the apprentice and the improver at the Bothy. The rest of the men walked to work from homes all over the estate, following established footpaths. The head gardener wore a top hat and tails, and was renowned for his lavender gloves!

A group of gardeners employed at Garnons by Sir John Cotterell, photographed in April 1909.

The Thomas family outside the Crown at Canon Pyon, c. 1904.

The Tram Inn, Eardisley, c. 1907, with a fine early motor car parked outside. This was the terminus of the tramway to Hay for a while. Later, the Kington tramway also ran from here – to the stone quarries beyond Kington.

Opposite above: The village street scene at Eardisley, c. 1906. This street runs for a quarter of a mile: a wonderful group of buildings with shops for every need, from cycles, bakers, grocers, to a coffee house.

Below: A postcard of High Street, Leominster, looking west, sent to a soldier in Ludlow in 1915. The card is slightly earlier in date, possibly around 1905.

Vicarage Street, Leominster, c. 1900. The fast flowing water rushing past their doors meant that the poorer people of the town who lived in the Lower Marsh, Knowle Street and Vicarage Street were less affected by typhoid than those in higher parts of the town, who drew water from the 444 wells in the town adjacent to cesspools. Water from the Pinsly was sold from barrels in the wealthier streets of Leominster.

An evocative photograph of a farmworker at Credenhill, who has been met by his son after work. The boy carries his father's costrell, a wooden cask used for carrying the daily cider ration to the fields. What happened to the house on the right? Any information would be very gratefully received.

Ross, Market House etc.

H.C. JEFFERIES

Above: Ross Market House, c. 1910, a meeting place for children not just on market day. Built around 1660–74 the Market House has been depicted on many postcards. Built of red sandstone, it is not timber framed like other Herefordshire market halls. The open arcaded ground floor has a fine hall above, which was used as the town hall in the past.

Left: John Kyrle's house, Ross-on-Wye, in 1911. The Man of Ross, John Kyrle, immortalized by Pope, was born in 1637. His life was described as 'one uninterrupted course of active and disinterested benevolence'. He died in 1724, and is buried in the church of St Mary the Virgin, where there is a fine monument in his memory. This postcard was published by H.C. Jeffries, late of Powle's Library, High Street, Ross.

Opposite above: Leominster Cottage Hospital in 1909, graced by two stalwart nurses in the doorway. Built in 1898 by public subscription, it opened with ten beds on 10 September 1899. Operations under anaesthesia did not begin until 1910, but twenty-five operations took place during the year. Scarlet fever patients were accommodated at the isolation hospital near Cursneh Hill, which opened in 1903.

Below: Broad Street, Ross, in 1905: wonderful shopfronts, with the Ross Coffee House on the left (with the flag), and on the right James Price & Sons, House Decorators. One can imagine the smells of tea and coffee from Bank House.

Above: Busy market day in Ledbury, c. 1905. Markets were held on a Tuesday, as today, but the stalls cluster closely around the Market Hall nowadays because of the modern two-way traffic.

Below: Ledbury Park, originally called New House, was built c. 1590 by the Hall family, clothiers from Lincolnshire. It is called by some the grandest black and white house in the county. Extended in 1820, there are extensive outbuildings and stables. The Hall family intermarried with the Biddulph family in the seventeenth century and remained here until the 1950s. During the Civil War, in 1646, Prince Rupert had his headquarters at the house when he routed Colonel Massey's forces. This card was sent in February 1903, when only the address was allowed on the reverse; so the message had to be written on the picture!

The bridge, Bosbury, a typical Edwardian view which was still on sale in the village in 1921. The writer mentions the 'Hop Club' created for hop workers, so they could write letters and relax after their labours.

The peaceful country churchyard at Bosbury, showing the preaching cross where Edna Lyall's ashes were buried in 1903. The Victorian bestseller's romantic novels were very popular, reflecting her own liberalism and passion for social reform. Gladstone praised them, and In the Golden Days was read to John Ruskin as he lay dying, the last book he enjoyed. Bosbury, where Edna's brother was the vicar, appears as the setting of her novel In Spite of All.

The Salmon Inn, at Bridge Sollars,
photographed c. 1880. This photograph of
the Prosser family, with Mr William Prosser,
the landlord, was taken by John Henry
Knight, an inventor and photographer from
Farnham, Surrey. From a banking family,
he travelled widely in the county, indulging
in his hobby of photography.

A delightful view of Mansell Lacy, c. 1890. The children pulling their cart over the bridge evoke a delightful summer's day with no school on the horizon.

Opposite above: The New Inn, Pembridge, seen here c. 1890. John Chandler, the landlord of the inn, is recorded as catering for the needs of weary cyclists and locals alike. It was a regular stopping point for the Cyclists Touring Club, and was very much the heart of the village. This photograph was also taken by John Henry Knight, who seems to have greatly admired half-timbered buildings.

Below: The Market House, Pembridge, c. 1900, a most useful wagon store. This timber-framed market hall dates from the early seventeenth century and may have had an upper storey. The carved posts are notched, possibly for displaying goods. The two stones on the east side are possibly 'nails' on which bargains were struck: the origins of 'paying on the nail'.

Annie Morris outside her cottage in Pembridge, c. 1890, everything neatly arranged beside her cottage door.

Opposite above: The organ man strolls through the Herefordshire countryside early this century, perhaps to play at a wedding or a wake. He was much in demand at village festivities across the county.

Below: The postman knocks at the door in Mansell Lacy, c. 1880. This is one of John Henry Knight's delightful photographs of the county.

THE OLD POST OFFICE,
CANON FFROME, NR. LEDBURY.

The delightful old post office at Canon Frome, near Ledbury, with its wonderful cottage garden. The young girls in the donkey cart look cool and comfortable in their sun bonnets. The sub-postmistress in 1900 was Mrs Ellen Reeves.

Bleak houses, known as The Barracks, at Kingsthorne. Further information would be welcome.

South Street, Leominster, in July 1907, site of the traditional horse fairs. The card was sent by a young girl called Alice to her sister, Miss Vaughan, saying that they were very busy: two meadows had been cut but she had five minutes free, so had chatted to a young farmer!

High Town, Hereford, c. 1900. A fine collection of horse-drawn vehicles including hansom cabs, leaving the cabbies' hut in front of the Old House. This cabbies' hut can still be seen today by the tennis courts on the Bishop's Meadow.

Above: Brian Hatton and his family at
Mount Craig in March 1907. This evocative
photograph records Edwardian family life.
Left to right: Marjorie Hatton, Mrs Hatton,
Ailsa Hatton, Brian himself. Brian often
painted his family and many versions of their
portraits can be seen in the Hatton Gallery,
at Churchill Gardens Museum, Venns Lane,
Hereford, together with delightful landscapes
of the county.

Right: Hereford artist Brian Hatton in
his studio at Mount Craig, Broomy Hill,
Hereford. Brian Hatton was a child prodigy,
his work was applauded from a very early age,
and he continued painting throughout his life
until his death in 1916 during the First World
War.

Above: Three small children in Credenhill on their way home from school in around 1905, beside the turning to Tillington. The cottages are still there today. The road behind the children leads on to RAF Hereford.

Left: The Great Oak at Eardisley, c. 1900. Marbles reigned supreme with most little boys at that date. The tree, on Hurstway Common, is approximately 30 ft in girth and over 100 ft high.

Little Birch School in 1935. Back row, left to right: M. Hodges, D. Evans, A. Hodges, F. Wooles, G. Monkley, D. Walker, N. Merrick, A. Jones. Middle row: H. Andrews, J. Cox, M. Powell, D. Monkley, J. Haines, G. Jones, P. Verry. Front row: G. Wooles, R. Morgan, D. Morgan, T. James, B. Morgan, F. Wooles, M. Cox, P. Morgan.

Tarrington School, c. 1892. This was taken by Savoury of Hereford. Mr Toyne, the headmaster, stands proudly with his charges. Among the children is Eric Toyne his son, and young Alice Griffiths.

Playtime at Canon Pyon School, c. 1900. It is interesting to note the girls playing together and the boys involved in a game of marbles. I don't think it would be a good idea to play in that very spot today! However, the school buildings are very much as they were in this fine photograph.

A splendid group of boys and girls from Bluecoat School lined up on Empire Day 1909, before marching to the Castle Green for celebrations and a special tea.

Above: Longtown schoolchildren who received silver medals for the third year running for perfect school attendance. These were presented by the Revd R.A. Kekewich and the vicar, G.V. Collinson.

Below: A formidable turn-out by the Herefordshire County Council Gymnasium Class for Ladies in April 1911. They often gave exhibitions of their prowess with clubs, dumb-bells and other somewhat vicious looking equipment. Apart from general fitness an element of self-defence was also taught, rather advanced for the period. Miss E.A. Love was the instructress.

Eign Street, Hereford, in the snow, c. 1900, a wonderful Dickensian Christmas card view.

Three

High Days and Holidays

Wilson's Annual Flower, Vegetable and Fruit Show in the Shire Hall, c. 1920. John Wilson instituted the show in 1898 and put up the prize money. Over a thousand entries were usually received and competition was severe in all classes: virtually the whole county visited or participated. Admission was free but donations were placed in hospital boxes to assist the City and the Cottage Hospitals. This annual show ceased at the start of the Second World War.

This photograph, dated 3 September 1864, shows the unveiling of the statue of Sir George Cornewall Lewis outside the Shire Hall, by Lord Palmerston, prime minister. Sir George had died in 1863 while still holding the office of secretary for war. Sir George was the MP for the County of Hereford 1847–52, chief steward of the city, chancellor of the exchequer 1855–8, home secretary 1859–60, then secretary for war 1860–3. The statue, still there today, is by Baron Marochetti. Hereford was crowded with people for the occasion and music was played by the Militia and Volunteer bands. The mayor and corporation walked in procession with Lord Palmerston to the Shire Hall before the ceremony. Afterwards Lord Palmerston lunched with the Bishop of Hereford and proceeded by the Great Western Railway back to London.

A busy sale of work at the Shire Hall in 1910, held under the auspices of the Hereford Liberals.

The maypole dance at Colwall Flower Show in August 1908.

The Queen of the May, a production at Kington performed by schoolchildren, in aid of Dr Barnardo's Homes, in April 1911.

Miss Jarley's Waxworks: a group who performed tableaux on a variety of themes at Ledbury Church Fancy Fair in July 1909.

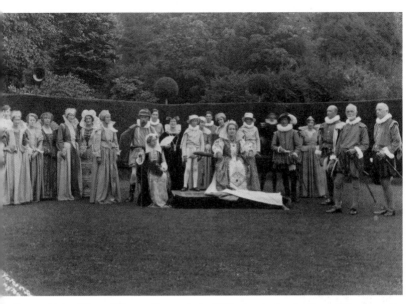

Above and below: Views of Kington Pageant in the 1920s. Any further details would be very welcome.

Above and below: Views of Kington Pageant in the 1920s. Again, any further details would be welcome. The City Museum would love a programme of this event, with its wonderful costumes and atmosphere.

Above: Stoke Lacy schoolchildren in their lavish production of *Blue Beard* in February 1911.

Below: An interesting photograph of the refreshment staff at Canon Pyon fête, on Club Walk day, 13 June 1912. Note the wonderful steam gallopers behind the staff.

Bosbury Horse and Flower Show, September 1907.

Ledbury Ploughing Society in 1907. Some of the committee pose for the record.

Opposite above: General Booth (on the left), founder of the Salvation Army, visited Ross-on-Wye in August 1908 (well wrapped up for motoring). Mr Southall, outside whose house, The Craig, Ross-on-Wye, this photograph was taken, is standing in the centre.

Below: The unveiling of the Stoke Edith horse trough by Lady Emily Foley in 1901. The much needed trough was sadly damaged a few years ago when it was hit by a van. It is now reconstructed and placed on the cobbles near the Old Rectory, and has been filled with flowers.

Sangers Circus parades through High Town, Hereford, c. 1880. The excited crowds would follow the circus to the racecourse where the big top had been erected. Local artist Brian Hatton painted the circus horses on a later visit.

May Fair in High Town, c. 1905. Particularly impressive is the showman's engine on the left. The crowds seem to be enjoying the sights and sounds of this splendid occasion.

Busy High Town during May Fair, c. 1900. The stalls and side shows are far more numerous than today; no wonder people came from all corners of the county to combine shopping with pleasure. Note the streetscape: the shops are very different today; and what happened to all those wonderful lamps?

Above: May Fair early morning, c. 1910. The shopkeepers' blinds have been set out already on what seems to be a glorious morning. No sign of 'May Fair weather', as Herefordians say.

Right: White's Tunnel at the May Fair at the end of the Boer War, c. 1902. It is rather close to the Shire Hall. Note the large advertisement for war pictures; a magic lantern show not to be missed.

The lifeboat procession passes Greenlands, High Town, Hereford in October 1908. Led by three horse-drawn fire engines, the lifeboat was pulled through the city and then launched from Castle Green into the river. The event raised a large amount of money for the RNLI and small cloth flags were sold. Organizations in the city often prepared floats for the annual Lifeboat Day, and a gentle competition ensued which added to the carnival atmosphere.

The 'Rhondda Pals' at Leominster, c. 1914. This group of men had volunteered for the army and were on an exercise at Leominster. Many units in the First World War were called the 'Pals', and this usually indicated that a group of miners had joined up at the same time, responding to their country's call.

Above and below: A rare pair of photographs of the Armistice declaration at Rotherwas Munition Works in 1918, taken outside the offices. Photographs were not often taken during the First or Second World Wars, so it is particularly interesting to locate these photographs.

Above: Alfred Watkins's fine photograph of a Herefordshire Volunteers fête taken in 1915 in the grounds of Vineyard Croft, Hampton Park, Hereford, where he lived for nearly thirty years. Watkins and his wife were great supporters of the war effort with fêtes and other events, which helped Herefordians to relax a little while supporting their 'boys' at home and abroad.

Below: A baby show at Yarpole in 1910. Frills and starched dresses and bonnets for boys and girls alike, while proud mamas gaze with mixed feelings. I can guess who won; can you?

A rare photograph of the interior of the Kemble Theatre, Broad Street, Hereford, laid out for a banquet, c. 1913. The staff of the Mitre Hotel check the last minute arrangements and pose by their efforts. The Mitre Hotel was across the road, now Knight Frank & Rutley, but sadly the Kemble Theatre was demolished in 1961.

Young and old enjoy skating on Huntington Pool in 1917.

The terrible fire in 1942 at St George's Hall, Hereford, the depot of the Hereford Motor Company, and next door to Bewell House and the brewery. The fire started during the night in Mr Jones's coach and the whole building was destroyed. It was thought a serviceman had dropped a cigarette which slowly smouldered and burst into flame. Originally the building had been a roller skating rink built for Charles Watkins. The building then became the brewery's hop and ale store when the roller skating craze was over. By 1892 it was the Monarch Mineral Water factory, and finally a garage and depot for coaches.

Bosbury Church. Partly destroyed by fire. July 12. 1917

Above: A dramatic postcard of Bosbury church, which was partly destroyed by fire on 12 July 1917. Sent in November of that year, the card comments on the fire and the rebuilding taking place at that time.

Right: The unfortunate sight of elm trees growing inside Ross church. Elms were planted in the churchyard by John Kyrle, but suckers came through the church walls into the church. The parent trees were cut down during the church restoration of 1878, and more elms were planted to the south of the church in 1899. The trees inside the church died, but their remains stood there until about 1953, when, riddled with woodworm, they were destroyed.

ROSS CHURCH - THE ELM TREES - 594

A motor accident in Hereford Road, Leominster, in April 1907. Cars were still a novelty at that time so an accident really caused crowds to gather. The car, registration number DAG 4, was driven by Mr E. Lisle of Wolverhampton. Passing a load of bricks he skidded and ran into the back. The driver, however, escaped unhurt.

A stable and cowhouse at Mr F.H.G. Cullere's Bridge House, Lugwardine. An elm fell in a terrible gale and crushed a stable. Fortunately the horse inside was rescued uninjured.

VOTE FOR CLIVE
AND SPEED THE PLOUGH.

Above: A postcard invitation to Captain Clive's public meeting, held to support his candidature for Parliament in June 1908. The Conservative candidate for South Herefordshire, Captain Clive and his wife seek the farming vote at the Trumpet ploughing match. He actively supported Herefordshire farming throughout his life and the slogan 'Speed the plough' is an ancient one, to be found on cottage mugs and jugs in the City Museum's collection. It must have appealed locally as the Captain, as he was known, was elected with a majority of over a thousand votes.

Right: Master John Arkwright, who actively supported his father, Mr J.S. Arkwright, in his election campaign to become MP for Hereford for the fourth time, in 1910.

Mr Austen Chamberlain leaving Whitfield Court after his visit to the county in 1910. From left to right: Chamberlain, Mrs P.A. Clive, Mrs Chamberlain and Captain P.A. Clive. The splendid chauffeur in a fine Mercedes awaits. The photo was taken by Croot Tucker of Hereford. The car was lent to assist the election effort. Mr G. Butcher drove Captain Clive on various occasions and was presented with a pair of gold cufflinks.

A sea of local people listen to the proclamation of King George V at Ledbury on 10 May 1910, by the Market Hall.

Above: A house party at the Garnons in February 1911. Standing, left to right: Miss Cecily Cotterell, the Hon. Mrs Denison, Mr Little, Miss Thornhill, Colonel Ricardo, Hon. Mrs Egerton, Lady Muriel Beckwith. Sitting: Lady Helen Gordon-Lennox, Miss Sylvia Cotterell, Miss Mildred Cotterell and Lady Cotterell. The fashionable clothes worn by this group are most interesting, as there are similar items in the collection at Churchill Gardens Museum.

Right: One of the Harding boys, who worked as a news boy in Hereford, displays the headlines during the Boer War. A keen photographer, Mr Harding Snr was trying out a new camera in August 1900. The America Cup refers to the first Davis Cup for tennis.

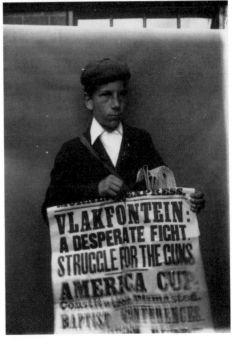

VLAKFONTEIN:
A DESPERATE FIGHT
STRUGGLE FOR THE GUNS
AMERICA CUP

Members of the Fownhope Heart of Oak Friendly Society prepare to set off on their annual walk, c. 1900. The club gathering took place on the nearest Sunday to Oak Apple Day, in May. The sticks are decorated with wooden apples and flowers, cut from cottage gardens, and carried in procession to the church for a service. The procession was preceded by the club banner, a band and an oak bough decorated with red, white and blue ribbons. A sprig of oak was also worn in memory of the escape of the Merry Monarch, King Charles II. The club walk still takes place on the first Saturday in June, and proceeds to the church.

Four

The Agricultural County

Herefordians at the London Dairy Show in 1907. The county was well represented and won many awards for butter and cheese making.

Students at the Herefordshire County Council Cheese and Dairy School at Wellington, in 1908.

This short-horn cow, the property of Messrs Shotton and R.P. Haden Cope of Bartestree Court, Hereford, gave birth to triplets, two bulls and a heifer. Four weeks old in the photograph, they were reared entirely by the mother. The live birth of triplets was a great rarity in 1909 and was the lead story in the Hereford Times on 27 February.

Milking at Fawley in 1932.

A charming photograph of a young lady posing in the doorway of a dairy at Hinton, in the early 1930s.

Champion Hereford bull Cameronian, which was bred by Captain E.L.A. Heygate of Buckland, Leominster, and was exported to South America by Messrs P. & G. Hughes. The splendid bull had an unbeaten show career, winning firsts on every occasion he was exhibited from 1904 onwards, including the championship at the Royal Show in 1906 and the Hereford & Worcester Show in 1907.

The first consignment of bacon pigs arriving in the county in the Commercial Autocar Company's motor van, pictured at the Hereford Slaughterhouses, as the abattoir was known, in 1909.

Above: A wonderful group of Ryeland sheep, the property of Mr F.E. Gough, Dinmore, Bodenham. Some of them won firsts in the Royal Show in 1909.

Sheep shearing at Norton Canon, c. 1900.

Pupils at the Herefordshire County Council poultry and dairy class at Wellington in 1911.

Opposite below: Sheep shearing competitions taking place at Urishay, Peterchurch, in July 1907. Top picture: hand-shearers' competition, with the boys' pens in the foreground, the men's sheep pens in the background. Bottom picture: the machine shearers, with the winners of the first prize on the right.

A horse-drawn wagon loads fruit at Burghill in August 1907, definitely a family affair as it still is today.

Mr Wallis's photograph of a new Herefordshire industry, in 1907, shows the first planting of 100,000 strawberry roots at Tillington Nurseries. Here women workers are digging up roots for orders of 1,000 plants at a time. It is interesting to see the prams parked by the rows. Now a great area of 'pick your own' strawberries, these were the first strawberries grown in the county, and the same fruit farm is very much part of local life today. Probably descendants of these workers are still cultivating the same land.

Haymakers at Holme Lacy, c. 1910. Some of these men were destined to leave the hay fields forever to go to the First World War.

A young boy helps with the reaping in the summer of 1932.

Binding barley in the country, possibly near Mordiford, c. 1910.

Above: The Bins at Longtown Mill, c. 1908

Right: Clodock Mill, c. 1900. The wheel was made in Leominster in 1868, and the mill is still in good order today.

Children hop picking in 1903: they seem very dedicated to their task. As soon as they could walk, children would help with the hops, a useful way to supplement the family income. Many spent a working holiday in Herefordshire, travelling there from their homes in Birmingham or the Black Country. The children here appear to be in their Sunday best.

Hop pickers at Ledbury in 1908.

Hop pickers at Newton, Dilwyn, in 1903. At the end of the day the hop cribs were emptied into pokes (sacks) as is happening here, then were taken to the kiln for the hops to be dried. Each bin was tallied and a token was given to be exchanged for pay, or goods. The tallyman stands behind the crib with his tally sticks, each one with a worker's name, which were notched when the bin was emptied.

A souvenir card from the Hop Gardens of Bosbury, written at Bosbury on 1 September 1921, and sent from a girl on holiday there: 'Having a lovely time. We go out about 10 into the fields and pick with the pickers until 12.45, then we have to get back for dinner, then rest after.' She also mentions the hop pickers' club, which opened from 7 to 10 p.m., with supper at 8 p.m.

A hop wagon outside the Foley Arms, Tarrington, in 1905, loaded with hop pockets (very large sacks). In July 1992 the pub was sold, and the name has been changed to the Glass Pig.

The cask yard at Hereford Brewery, c. 1890, owned by the Watkins family. They sold their empire of thirty-five hotels and public houses and the brewery in 1898 to the Tredegar Brewing Company, which later became Hereford & Tredegar Brewery Ltd.

The stalwart workers at Ross Malthouse, c. 1911.

A fruit and flower show at the Shire Hall in 1895. This is the stand of the National Association of Cider Makers, which was founded in 1894. This display, by Mr John Watkins of Withington, has a bewildering number of different types of cider apple, all clearly labelled, and many more varieties than can be found today.

A large portable rotary cider mill, or scratter, on a farm near Longtown, c. 1920. In the background there is a double screw press. The scratter mill could handle about a hundred bushels of apples per hour. The pig in the foreground is enjoying the spoiled must, or crushed pulp. The man in the picture is probably a travelling cider maker, who would go from farm to farm with his scatter and press to assist farmers who did not have their own 'tack' (equipment).

Apple tumps being loaded at Pomona Farm, Withington, c. 1900. These heaps of cider apples were covered with straw in order to help mellow the apples, and concentrate the sugars in the juice as the fruit lost moisture. The farm was owned by John Watkins, brother of Alfred Watkins.

Alfred Watkins's photograph of bee-keeping, c. 1890. The fine frame hives indicate that perhaps he was a member of the Herefordshire Beekeepers Association, who had dispensed with the old straw bee skeps that resulted in the death of the bees when the honey was taken. Funded by the County Council, a horse-drawn bee van toured the county to teach efficiency and good bee-keeping practice.

John Wilson, Florist & Seedsman. This is his first shop, in Commercial Street, photographed around 1908. The shop was opposite the present premises, which were built in 1915.

A splendid display of Cranston's Excelsior onions on the right, at Wilson's Horticultural Show in September 1910. Very much a focal part of Herefordshire life up to the Second World War, this show was judged by Messrs Biggs, Liddle, Jones, McCormack, Harden, Palliser, Roberts and Parry.

Above: Clog makers at work in Hill Dingle, Dorstone, c. 1900.

Left: Hurdle making at Mordiford, in 1922. Many villagers had a hurdle maker who specialized in gate hurdles for shepherds, which had to be light and easily moved.

Opposite above: Women workers on the land in Herefordshire during the First World War. They are sawing and stacking timber with great energy. Any further information would be very welcome concerning these spirited ladies.

Below: The wheelwright shop at Pembridge in 1930. The wheelwright was Mr William Breakwell.

The saw mill at Pontrilas, shown here in 1937. It is still very prominent in the village today.

A blacksmith works in the courtyard of Brinsop Court, an important early fourteenth-century moated manor house with sixteenth-, seventeenth- and eighteenth-century additions. Much restored in 1913 for the Astley family, it was later the home of film star Madeleine Carroll and her husband, Captain Philip Astley.

The blacksmith's forge, Brookside, Canon Pyon, c. 1904.

Leominster Horse Fair, c. 1905, in South Street, originally called Turnbull Street, usually held on 4 September. People from all over the county came to this horse fair but the building of the cattle and sheep market in 1908, in Dishley Street, by Messrs Cooper & Baldwin, Auctioneers, meant that the horse sales also moved there.

A novel agricultural 'lorry' built in October 1912, with caterpillar tracks. Invented by Mr Beamond of Sutton Coldfield, it was tried out on several county farms without great success.

Above: An unusual wagon with solid wheels, photographed in the county c. 1928 by the late F.C. Morgan, former librarian and curator and keen photographer. His fine collection of negatives can be found in the City Library. Note the splendid hedge laying, behind the cart.

Right: Farmer William Mullow, of Marston Common, photographed c. 1850, some twenty years before his death. He is wearing the full farmer's outfit for the period, including corduroy trousers and leather leggings, very similar to some in the museum's collection.

124

A comprehensive photograph of the Christmas Market, 1939, in the Butter Market, Hereford. Many well known people can be found here. This market, the first of the war, was perhaps the last chance for the full dressed-poultry market, when people came from all over the county to purchase their poultry for Christmas. The photographer stood on top of Smiths Toy Stall at the end of the Butter Market to picture this scene.

A novel way of growing vegetable marrows over an arch. These were grown by Mr H. Gains, Lower Bullingham, Hereford, in the summer of 1910. The feat was duly reported in the *Hereford Times*.

This fine photograph was taken on 14 July 1913, by Miss Gladstone, showing Bernard Jones and his father David Jones at White House Farm, Tupsley.

Five

Sport and Leisure

Much Marcle football team in 1911.

Hereford Road Cycling Club pose in 1908, before setting out on an expedition.

The renowned hockey team at Miss Earle's School, Hereford, photographed in August 1908.
This Unwin photograph shows standing, left to right: Miss Mercer (coach), H. Damsell, E. Cox,
M. Dallow, Miss W. Earle (secretary). Kneeling: V. Powell, H. Wilson, G. Hone. Sitting: Miss M.
Pudge, M. Siversten, G. Phillips, M. Hislop (captain), G. Powell. Note the smart caps!

Opposite below: A presentation to Mr H.G. Farrant by the Ledbury Hunt. Mr Farrant of Welland
was presented with a painting of his favourite horse, Redhall, which won the National Hunt
Steeplechase at Warwick in 1907. Mr Farrant regularly hunted Redhall with the Ledbury Hounds
and the painting was the work of Mrs Fox, a well known animal painter whose work 'The Last
Fence' had attracted considerable attention at the Royal Academy Summer Exhibition in 1906. The
Hereford Times informs us that 'this work was painted from life, of course.' The Hunt presented
the painting to record the achievement of winning £1,000, and assured Mr Farrant 'that it betoken
our warmest appreciation'.

Above: The pre-Christmas meet of Ledbury Hounds at Eastnor Castle in December 1908.

The new green and pavilion of the Kington Bowling Club, shown at the opening ceremony tea in August 1910.

The new croquet and lawn tennis grounds at Ross, c. 1910.

Opposite above: Cricket at Stoke Edith. These two photographs, by H. Pattison, record a famous match in September 1907. This is the Hon. Miss Leigh's XI. Back row, left to right: Mrs Butler, D. Leigh, Revd Mr Leveson-Gower, Mrs Leigh, R.F. Bailey, H. Charrington, Dr Higgins. Centre row: G. Bosworth Smith, H.R.G. Leveson-Gower, G.A. Denny, E.G.M. Carmichael. Front row: G.G. Napier, J. Douglas, R.P. Keigwin, Captain Butler.

Below: P.H. Foley's XI. Back row, left to right: Mrs Foley, Miss Wilkinson, Mrs B. Davenport, Miss Romilly, Miss Foster Hunt. Centre row: the Hon. C. Lyttelton, Revd C. Robinson, H.K. Foster, ? Braithwaite, W.B. Burns, H. Bromley Davenport, A.M. Miller, P. Bradstock. Front row: P. Foley, F.W. Romney, G. Robinson, W.S. Bird.

Ross Cricket Club in 1908.

Eardisley Quoit Club in 1909. Quoits was very popular throughout the county before the First World War. Standing, left to right: W. Gummer, W. Philpotts, C. Philpotts, -?-. Seated: J. Southgate, W. Cartwright (secretary), J. Elemont and son, J. Watkins (captain).

The Townsend family pose for a photograph, perhaps about to go on an outing, c. 1890. A tandem, tricycles and the splendid penny farthings perhaps await a customer, as the Townsends had a bicycle shop at 24 High Town, Hereford.

Herbert (Mickey) Minton, the champion Hereford cyclist with his trophies in 1907. As an amateur, he achieved two world records, four MCU championships, won numerous cups and acquired 200 first, 140 second and 180 third prizes.

This wonderful motorcycle was built in 1909 by James Fryer, Borough Motor Works, Leominster, to the design of one of his engineers Mr H.G. Munro. It was described as a 'novel' motorcycle, built entirely on car lines, there being no forks. The front wheel is carried on a swivel pin and coupled to the steering column by a rod with ball-jointed ends. The wheelbase was 63 in and the wheels measured 26 in by 2 ¼ in. The engine was taken from an old tricycle and was a 2 ¼ hp De Dion Bouton; the drive to the rear wheel was by 2 in Ralata flat belt. There was a Longuemare carburettor, and ignition by Hellesen dry-cell and special coil, which took one fifth of an amp current. The saddle was very low, being only 26½ in from the ground, which ensured great safety in 'greasy' weather. The long wheelbase made the machine very comfortable and free from vibration. Stout footrests were fitted low down to protect the machine in case of a fall. All the control was entirely from the handle-bars by means of Bowden wires, auto-lock levers and Chater Lea thumbslides. The machine was in daily use and was driven long distances.

The Herefordshire Golf Club Team Championship, c. 1957, at Herefordshire Golf Club, Wormsley. The back rows include Dr McGinn, A.D. Evans, Mr Jaques, H. Porter, E. Francis, L. Griffith, E.L. Evans, C. Ovend, S. Austin, A. Dyer, G. Heins, W. Plant, Dr Jones Roberts, F.D.V. Cant, D. Smith, G. Lane and G. Grubb. Front row, left to right: J. McLean (Lord Lieutenant), Mrs Davenport, Major Davenport, P. Peacock, C. Griffith. The captain was Mr Phillip.

Six

Transport

On Leominster station in 1911 emigrants pose, perhaps nervously, before setting out for a new life in Canada. Well wrapped up and full of hope, they prepare to set out to sail by the SS *Lake Champlain*. F. Dalley, the shipping agent of Leominster, arranged the passage.

Above: The Great Western Railway's Peterchurch station, on the line from Pontrilas to Hay-on-Wye, c. 1912. No trains ran on a Sunday but four ran each way on weekdays.

The Station, Ledbury

Busy Ledbury station, c. 1910, viewed from Dog Hill, above the tunnel. The station has changed very much today, with only the signal box and footbridge remaining. This postcard, by Tilly, was printed in Bavaria.

Opposite below: The station bus awaits customers at Ledbury station in 1909. The writer of the card identifies 'Edwin on the horse, but his cap is large.' Today the main station buildings have gone but the station-master's house remains.

Lady Cornewall, of Moccas Court, cuts the first sod of the Golden Valley Railway on 31 August 1876. The City Museum possesses the fine solid silver spade presented to her on this auspicious occasion. The railway was opened from Pontrilas in 1881, and terminated at Dorstone. It was extended to Hay eight years later. The 18¼ miles of railway cost £300,000 and the company hardly made a profit. It only possessed one locomotive, two coaches and a brake van, and rented other rolling stock as necessary. The passenger services ceased in 1941 and the line finally closed in 1957, the sad loss of such a beautiful route.

Ross railway station in June 1909, with a train in the Monmouth bay. The Hereford, Ross and Monmouth Railway, 36¹/₂ miles in length, received Royal Assent in 1845.

H.C. Cook's fine photo of a very nasty accident at Kington in 1909. The traction engine skidded and knocked down the side of the bridge, and was pulled out of its precarious position just in time!

Above and below: These two photographic postcards show the first flying machine in the county in April 1912. Mr Corbett Wilson landed his Blériot monoplane at Newchurch, near Weobley, to effect urgent repairs. Crowds rushed to the scene to examine the plane. Wilson was a fairly inexperienced pilot who had a wager with his friend Mr Allen to race to Dublin from Hendon aerodrome, a distance of 140 miles, in two hours. Sadly, Mr Allen was lost with his plane in the Irish Sea, an early casualty of 'flying mania', as it was called at the time.

This is probably the opening of Fryers Garage, Leominster, which was pulled down in the 1960s. CJ 270 is a 16/20 Humber belonging to T. Oram, Cagebrook Mill; H 2550 is a Wolseley/Siddeley; CJ 183 is an 8 hp Alldays & Onions belonging to T.A. King, Hereford. CJ 284 is a 20 hp Darracq, belonging to Mrs Williams of Kingsland; CJ 261 is a 10/12 hp Humber belonging to J.H. Nott of Leominster. James Fryer is in the back of CJ 270.

A group of cars taken outside Lyston Court c. 1907. From left to right: a 20 hp Darracq Tourer belonging to Mr A. Darcy of Clifton and later of Copelands (Holmer, Hereford); CJ 219, a 10/12 hp Clement Talbot four-seater owned by Mr J.W.W. Smith of Aramstone, Hoarwithy; E 503 is possibly a Clement registered in Staffordshire; CJ 376 is a 15 hp Humber Tourer (green) belonging to Major G.W. Davey of Lyston Court, Llanwarne; Y 71 was registered to G.W. Davey of Stoke Bishop, Bristol – a 30 hp Humber. Major Davey had a fine collection of cars and was a very keen early motorist. His chauffeur was Mr Wilson, who must have thoroughly enjoyed working with the cars.

An interesting view of the shopfront of S.T. Owen, the cycle and motor repairer, also known as the Owen Cycle Works, in St Owen Street. Sydney Thomas Owen was at No. 124 St Owen Street between 1900 and 1905. Outside the shop, a Minerva motorcycle is leaning against a wall; this motorcycle was registered in 1904. The wicker trailer is quite attractive and the tricycle is possibly one that Owen made himself. The shop was known for its penny farthing bicycle suspended on a bracket above the shop, just visible here.

Tarrington village in 1906. Situated in the centre of the hop yards, the wagons laden with hop pockets were a familiar autumn sight.

Mr Newman, the gamekeeper for the Hampton Court estate, photographed in Corn Square, Leominster by Mr Jones of Middle Marsh during the late 1860s.

Seven

The River

A view of Symonds Yat, sent by Mr Alfred Bird, builder, of Wye Street, Ross-on-Wye, to a member of the Hearts of Oak delegation. This card was specially overprinted for him in 1911.

The Harding family picnic by the river, c. 1890: an afternoon of recreation, fishing, cycling or just enjoying the scenery. Mr Harding seems to be in charge of the picnic.

A view of Jordan's Boatyard by the Wye Bridge, Hereford, c. 1890. The yacht is a rare sight. Further details about it and its owner would be very welcome.

The boat house at Bridge Sollars, c. 1900, a favourite spot for a walk. Early cyclists came out from Hereford to enjoy the views and to picnic on the river bank.

The Rowing Club house, c. 1880, at Ross-on-Wye, built by Mr E. Kendall Pearson.

Mr Parker's steamboat takes members of the Hatton family of Hereford on a trip to Belmont, in 1892.

ROSS FROM THE RIVER

A fine view of Ross-on-Wye across the river, c. 1910. On the left is the Wilton Castle, a stern-wheeled paddle steamer launched by Ross boat builders Henry Dowell and Son on Wyeside in May 1902. It could take 100 passengers and travel at 8 miles an hour. Used for pleasure trips for many years, it eventually decayed and was destroyed.

Opposite: Mr William Dew the coracle maker, photographed with one of his coracles c. 1900, near his premises at Kerne Bridge. The City Museum has the last of the Wye coracles in its collection.

Kerne Bridge, c. 1910. This delightful stretch of river was used for testing coracles made by William Dew.

Victoria Bridge, Hereford, almost disappearing in the great flood of 17 December 1910. Photographed at 16 ft, the water rose slightly higher.

Right: St Martin's Street, Hereford did not escape the floods either, this time in December 1916.

Below: Recreation on the Wye in February 1917. The freezing weather enabled skating to be enjoyed for several weeks.

Summer in Hereford, c. 1905. The River Wye today still seems dangerously attractive in hot weather to many young people.

The ferry at Symonds Yat near Whitchurch in 1894. This area has been visited by tourists since the late eighteenth century. Note the fine Wye trow in the foreground and the Ferry Inn nearby, still a place of enjoyment for visitors today.

Whitchurch Ferry.

3520 B.

Whitchurch ferry, c. 1905, a very well used crossing of the River Wye. Victorian and Edwardian ladies and gentlemen could also hire boats to admire the magnificent scenery at this point.

Members of the Hatton family pushing themselves out of trouble in the shallows near Breinton, in around 1900.

Above: Dr S.S. Wesley's fishing knife, presented to Dr G.R. Sinclair, organist of Hereford Cathedral in 1909. The photograph was taken by Gus Edwards especially for the Musical Times. Dr Wesley enjoyed fishing in Winchester just as much as Dr Sinclair enjoyed fishing at Hereford. Wesley thought nothing of deciding to be unavoidably detained while on his way to teach music; in fact he stopped off at any interesting stretch of river and stayed put for the day. His fishing equipment usually accompanied him whenever he went out in his dog cart.

Right: A young member of the Hatton family proudly poses with his prize pike, photographed by his father c. 1910.

A wonderful view from the Iron Age hill fort at Dinedor looking towards the City of Hereford, c. 1908. In the foreground is the Dinedor Tea Garden, a favourite afternoon outing for Herefordians in the days before the First World War.

Acknowledgements

I welcome the opportunity to express my thanks to the many who have assisted me in the compilation of this book and for the sharing of their knowledge, especially Hereford City Library (Mr B.J. Whitehouse and Mr R. Hill) and Hereford City Council for the use of many photographs from their respective collections. Similarly I am extremely grateful for advice and the loan of material from the following:

Miss E. Hill • Miss J. Wilson • Mrs D. Stallard • Mr E. Hatton • Mrs M. Rees
Mrs N. Palmer • Mrs M. Welham • Mr J. McKee • Mr B. Butcher
Mrs D. Coleman • Mr & Mrs W.G. Jones • Mr D. Foxton • Sir John Cotterell
Mr & Mrs A. Finney • Mr R. Shoesmith • Mrs S. Badham.

Every effort has been made to ascertain photographic copyright, where appropriate.
Very special thanks are due to Mrs F. Powell, Mr K. Hoverd, Mr J. Koenigsbeck and finally my husband, David Berry, for all his help and encouragement.